contents

NZ, Canada, US and UK readers
Please note that Australian cup and spoon measurements are metric. A quick conversion guide appears on page 63.

baked eggs with ham and cheese

50g shaved ham, chopped coarsely
2 green onions, sliced finely
4 eggs
⅓ cup (40g) coarsely grated cheddar

Preheat oven to moderate (180°C/160°C fan-forced). Grease four ½-cup (125ml) ovenproof dishes.
Divide ham and onion among dishes. One at a time, break eggs into small bowl, carefully sliding egg from bowl over ham and onion in each dish. Sprinkle dishes with equal amounts of cheese.
Place dishes on oven tray; bake, uncovered, about 10 minutes or until yolks are just set.

serves 4
per serving 9.1g fat; 540kJ (129 cal)
tip By breaking the eggs into a small bowl first, you will be able to discard any bad eggs without ruining the other ingredients in the dish. By sliding the egg carefully into the dish, it is less likely to splash.

mushroom, capsicum and cheese omelettes

You can make the vegetable filling a little ahead of time, but only make the omelettes just before you want to serve them. We used button mushrooms for our omelettes, but you can choose any variety you like.

20g butter
1 small red capsicum (150g), sliced thinly
200g mushrooms, sliced thinly
2 tablespoons finely chopped fresh chives
8 eggs
1 tablespoon milk
4 green onions, sliced thinly
½ cup (60g) coarsely grated cheddar

Melt butter in large frying pan; cook capsicum, mushroom and chives, stirring occasionally, about 4 minutes or until vegetables soften. Drain vegetable filling on absorbent-paper-lined plate; cover with foil to keep warm.
One at a time, break eggs into small bowl, then pour into large jug. When all eggs are in jug, whisk until well combined and frothy, then whisk in milk and onion.
Pour half of the egg mixture into the frying pan you used for the vegetables; tilt pan to cover base with egg mixture. Cook over medium heat about 4 minutes or until omelette is just set.
Carefully spoon half the vegetable filling onto one half of the omelette; sprinkle half of the cheese over vegetable filling. Use a spatula to lift and fold the unfilled half over the vegetable filling. Carefully slide omelette onto plate; cover with foil to keep warm.
Make one more omelette with remaining egg mixture, vegetable filling and cheese. Cut each omelette in half; place one half on each serving plate.

serves 4
per serving 20.1g fat; 1132kJ (270 cal)

porridge with apple and pear compote

3½ cups (875ml) hot water
1½ cups (135g) rolled oats
½ cup (125ml) milk

apple and pear compote

1 large apple (200g), chopped coarsely
1 medium pear (230g), chopped coarsely
⅓ cup (80ml) apple juice
1 tablespoon lemon juice

Make apple and pear compote.
Combine the water and oats in medium saucepan over medium heat; cook, stirring, about 5 minutes or until porridge is thick and creamy. Stir in milk.
Serve topped with apple and pear compote.
apple and pear compote Combine ingredients in medium saucepan; bring to a boil. Reduce heat; simmer, covered, stirring occasionally, about 15 minutes or until fruit softens and liquid is absorbed.

serves 4
per serving 4.2g fat; 853kJ (204 cal)
tip To prepare porridge in a microwave oven, combine the water and oats in large microwave-safe bowl, cover; cook on HIGH (100%) for 2 minutes, then pause and stir. Cook again, covered, on HIGH (100%) for 3½ minutes, then pause and stir. Cover; stand 5 minutes, then stir in milk.

honey-roasted muesli

¾ cup (60g) rolled oats
½ cup (55g) rolled rye
½ cup (55g) rolled rice
¼ cup (15g) unprocessed wheat bran
½ cup (175g) honey
1 tablespoon vegetable oil
⅓ cup (40g) coarsely chopped walnuts
¼ cup (40g) pepitas
1 teaspoon ground cinnamon
⅓ cup (50g) coarsely chopped dried apricots
⅓ cup (30g) coarsely chopped dried apples
¼ cup (40g) raisins

Preheat oven to moderate (180°C/160°C fan-forced).
Combine oats, rye, rice and bran in medium baking dish; drizzle evenly with honey and oil. Roast, uncovered, 5 minutes; stir, roast, uncovered, further 10 minutes.
Remove from oven; stir in remaining ingredients. Serve with milk or yogurt.

serves 4
per serving 18.1g fat; 2218kJ (530 cal)
tips You can double or triple the quantity of ingredients and store muesli in an airtight container in refrigerator for up to three months. The muesli is delicious topped with fresh seasonal fruit.

buttermilk pancakes with glazed strawberries

4 eggs
2 tablespoons caster sugar
1½ cups (375ml) buttermilk
100g butter, melted
1½ cups (225g) self-raising flour

glazed strawberries

⅓ cup (80ml) water
½ cup (170g) marmalade
1 tablespoon caster sugar
2 tablespoons lemon juice
250g strawberries, quartered

Beat eggs and sugar in small bowl with electric mixer until thick; stir in buttermilk and half of the butter.
Sift flour into large bowl; whisk egg mixture gradually into flour until batter is smooth.
Make glazed strawberries.
Heat heavy-based medium frying pan; brush pan with a little of the remaining butter. Pour ¼ cup of the batter into pan; cook, uncovered, until bubbles appear on surface of pancake. Turn pancake; cook until browned. Remove from pan; cover to keep warm. Repeat with remaining butter and batter.
Serve pancakes with glazed strawberries.
glazed strawberries Place the water, marmalade, sugar and juice in small saucepan; bring to a boil. Add strawberries, reduce heat; simmer, uncovered, about 2 minutes or until strawberries are hot.

serves 4
per serving 28.5g fat; 2810kJ (671 cal)

caramelised banana and hazelnut waffles

4 packaged Belgian-style waffles
40g butter
4 ripe bananas (800g), sliced thickly
2 tablespoons brown sugar
½ cup (75g) roasted hazelnuts, chopped coarsely
⅓ cup (80ml) maple syrup

Preheat oven to moderately slow (170°C/150°C fan-forced).
Place waffles, in single layer, on oven tray; cook, uncovered, about 8 minutes, just to heat through.
Meanwhile, melt butter in medium frying pan; cook banana, stirring, about 2 minutes or until hot. Add sugar; cook, uncovered, over low heat, about 2 minutes or until banana is caramelised lightly.
Divide waffles among serving plates; top with banana mixture, nuts and syrup.

serves 4
per serving 27.2g fat; 2283kJ (545 cal)
tip Nuts can be omitted from recipe, if desired.

hummus and cucumber

Spread one slice of bread with 1 tablespoon prepared hummus; top with a quarter of a thinly sliced lebanese cucumber and another slice of bread.

per sandwich 4.9g fat; 700kJ (167 cal)

fruit and nut

Spread one slice of bread with 3 teaspoons hazelnut chocolate spread, then top with 1 tablespoon sultanas and half of a thinly sliced small banana. Top with another slice of bread.

per sandwich 6.2g fat; 1194kJ (285 cal)

chicken, avocado and cream cheese

Combine ¼ cup (40g) coarsely chopped barbecued chicken meat, a quarter of a coarsely chopped small avocado and 1 teaspoon lemon juice in small bowl. Spread 1 tablespoon spreadable cream cheese over one slice of bread; top with chicken mixture, ¼ cup loosely packed mixed salad leaves, and another slice of bread.

per sandwich 19.2g fat; 1417kJ (338 cal)

egg, tomato and mayonnaise

Combine half of a seeded, finely chopped small tomato, 1 tablespoon coarsely grated cheddar cheese, one coarsely chopped hard-boiled egg and 1 tablespoon mayonnaise in small bowl. Spread mixture over one slice of bread; top with ¼ cup loosely packed mixed lettuce leaves and another slice of bread.

per sandwich 16.6g fat; 1259kJ (301 cal)

tuna and sweet corn

Combine half of a drained 185g can tuna in spring water, 2 tablespoons drained and rinsed canned sweet corn kernels and 1 tablespoon mayonnaise in small bowl. Spread mixture over one slice of bread. Top with a quarter of a thinly sliced lebanese cucumber and another slice of bread.

per sandwich 9.6g fat; 1276kJ (305 cal)

peanut butter and vegies

Spread 1 tablespoon peanut butter over two slices of bread; top one slice with 1 tablespoon coarsely grated carrot and 1 tablespoon coarsely grated celery. Top with remaining bread slice.

per sandwich 13.9g fat; 1127kJ (269 cal)

cheese and vegies

Combine 2 tablespoons coarsely grated cheddar cheese, 2 tablespoons coarsely grated carrot, 2 tablespoons coarsely grated celery and 1 tablespoon sour cream in small bowl. Spread mixture over one slice of bread; top with another slice of bread.

per sandwich 16.1g fat; 1227kJ (293 cal)

cheese, sausage and pickle

Spread 1 tablespoon of sweet mustard pickle over two slices of bread; top one slice of bread with one slice of cheddar cheese and one cold cooked thickly sliced beef sausage. Top with remaining slice of bread.

per sandwich 21.3g fat; 1454kJ (347 cal)

thai beef salad

500g beef rump steak

60g bean thread noodles

1 lebanese cucumber (130g), halved lengthways, seeded, sliced thinly

100g cherry tomatoes, quartered

1 small red capsicum (150g), sliced thinly

3 green onions, sliced thinly

⅓ cup firmly packed fresh coriander leaves

⅓ cup firmly packed fresh mint leaves

thai dressing

¼ cup (60ml) lemon juice

1 tablespoon fish sauce

1 tablespoon brown sugar

1 tablespoon peanut oil

Cook beef in heated oiled large frying pan until browned on both sides and cooked as desired. Cover; stand 10 minutes, then slice beef thinly.

Meanwhile, place noodles in large heatproof bowl, cover with boiling water, stand until just tender; drain. Using kitchen scissors, cut noodles into random lengths.

Make thai dressing.

Return noodles to same cleaned bowl with remaining ingredients and dressing; toss gently to combine.

thai dressing Place ingredients in screw-top jar; shake well.

serves 4

per serving 8.2g fat; 1130kj (270 cal)

minestrone

Many varieties of already-cooked white beans are available canned, among them cannellini, butter and haricot beans; they are all suitable for this soup. You can use any small pasta, such as little shells, small macaroni or even risoni.

1 tablespoon olive oil
1 small brown onion (80g), chopped finely
1 clove garlic, crushed
2 bacon rashers (140g), rind removed, chopped finely
1 trimmed celery stalk (100g), grated coarsely
2 medium carrots (240g), grated coarsely
410g can crushed tomatoes
2 cups (500ml) beef stock
1 litre (4 cups) water
½ cup (65g) short pasta
2 medium zucchini (240g), grated coarsely
300g can white beans, rinsed, drained
⅓ cup thinly sliced fresh basil

Heat oil in large saucepan; cook onion, garlic, bacon and celery, stirring, about 5 minutes or until vegetables just soften.
Add carrot, undrained tomato, stock, the water and pasta; bring to a boil. Reduce heat; simmer, covered, about 5 minutes or until pasta is just tender.
Add zucchini and beans; bring to a boil. Remove from heat; stir in basil.

serves 4
per serving 8.1g fat; 904kJ (216 cal)

vegetable and fetta free-form tarts

1 small eggplant (230g), chopped coarsely

coarse cooking salt

1 tablespoon olive oil

1 medium brown onion (150g), sliced thinly

2 medium zucchini (240g), sliced thinly

4 sheets ready-rolled short crust pastry

¼ cup (65g) bottled pesto

120g piece fetta, crumbled

8 cherry tomatoes, halved

1 tablespoon finely chopped fresh basil

1 egg, beaten lightly

Place eggplant in sieve or colander; sprinkle all over with salt; stand 15 minutes. Rinse eggplant, drain; pat dry with absorbent paper.

Preheat oven to moderate (180°C/160°C fan-forced).

Heat oil in large non-stick frying pan; cook onion, stirring, until softened. Add eggplant and zucchini, stirring, until vegetables soften.

Using a plate as a guide, cut a 20cm round from each pastry sheet; place rounds on oven trays. Spread equal amounts of pesto in centre of each round, leaving a 4cm border around outside edge.

Divide vegetables among rounds over pesto; top each with equal amounts of cheese, tomato and basil. Using hands, turn 4cm edge on each round over filling; brush around pastry edge with egg. Bake, uncovered, about 40 minutes or until pastry is browned lightly.

serves 4

per serving 57.8g fat; 3570kJ (853 cal)

tip Allowing the eggplant to stand while covered with salt will help remove most of the vegetable's slightly bitter juice; it also helps prevent the eggplant from absorbing too much oil when it's cooked. Be sure to rinse the eggplant well under cold running water to remove as much of the salt as possible, and dry it thoroughly with absorbent paper before cooking.

pasta and chicken salad

Penne is an Italian word for the old-fashioned quill pen, a tool which this ridged macaroni, cut into short lengths on the diagonal, resembles. You can use any small pasta – macaroni, fusilli or farfalle – that you like instead of penne.

600g chicken breast fillets
250g penne
1 large red capsicum (350g), chopped coarsely
4 large egg tomatoes (360g), seeded, chopped coarsely
6 green onions, sliced thinly
200g piece fetta, chopped coarsely
80g baby rocket leaves

vinaigrette

¼ cup (60ml) olive oil
⅓ cup (80ml) red wine vinegar
1 teaspoon dijon mustard
1 teaspoon sugar

Place chicken in medium saucepan, cover with boiling water; return to a boil. Reduce heat; simmer, uncovered, about 10 minutes or until cooked through. Cool chicken, still in poaching liquid, 10 minutes. Remove chicken from pan, slice thickly; discard poaching liquid.
Meanwhile, cook pasta in medium saucepan of boiling water until just tender; drain. Rinse under cold water; drain.
Make vinaigrette.
Place chicken and pasta in large bowl with remaining ingredients and vinaigrette; toss gently to combine.
vinaigrette Place ingredients in screw-top jar; shake well.

serves 4
per serving 29.9g fat; 2877kJ (687 cal)

fried rice

1 tablespoon peanut oil
2 eggs, beaten lightly
120g baby corn, halved
1 trimmed celery stalk (100g), chopped finely
1 small red capsicum (150g), chopped finely
2 cloves garlic, crushed
140g ham, chopped coarsely
3 cups cooked long-grain white rice
1 tablespoon kecap manis
4 green onions, sliced thinly

Heat half of the oil in wok. Add egg, swirl to cover base of wok; cook until set. Remove omelette from wok, roll up tightly; cut omelette into thin slices.
Heat remaining oil in wok; stir-fry corn and celery 2 minutes. Add capsicum, garlic and ham; stir-fry 2 minutes.
Add rice and kecap manis; stir-fry until heated through. Stir in onion and omelette.

serves 4
per serving 9.4g fat; 1409kJ (337 cal)

oven-baked chicken schnitzel with wedges

1kg potatoes
1 egg white, beaten lightly
½ teaspoon sweet paprika
4 chicken thigh fillets (440g)
⅓ cup (50g) plain flour
2 egg whites, beaten lightly, extra
½ cup (35g) packaged breadcrumbs
½ cup (80g) corn flake crumbs
1 teaspoon garlic salt

Preheat oven to hot (220°C/220°C fan-forced).

Cut unpeeled potatoes into wedges. Combine potato, egg white and paprika in large bowl; toss to coat potato all over in spice mixture.

Place potato, in single layer, in lightly oiled shallow baking dish; bake, uncovered, about 40 minutes or until browned lightly.

Meanwhile, trim fat from chicken. Using meat mallet, gently pound chicken between sheets of plastic wrap until 5mm thick. Toss chicken in flour; shake away excess. Dip chicken in small bowl containing extra egg white, then toss in separate small bowl containing combined crumbs and salt.

Place chicken, in single layer, on oiled oven tray; bake, uncovered, about 20 minutes or until browned both sides and cooked through.

Halve chicken schnitzels and serve with wedges.

serves 4

per serving 10.1g fat; 1965kJ (470 cal)

tips If you prefer, use stale breadcrumbs flavoured with grated lemon rind and finely chopped parsley in place of the corn flake crumbs.

Serve chicken schnitzels with lime wedges, a bowl of thai sweet chilli sauce and a green salad dressed with lemon vinaigrette, if desired.

rissoles with cabbage mash

2 bacon rashers (140g), chopped finely
1 small brown onion (80g), chopped finely
1 tablespoon worcestershire sauce
1 cup (70g) stale breadcrumbs
1 egg
¼ cup coarsely chopped fresh parsley
500g beef mince
2 tablespoons barbecue sauce
2 cups (500ml) beef stock
1 tablespoon cornflour
2 tablespoons water

cabbage mash

1kg potatoes, quartered
¼ cup (60ml) milk
20g butter, chopped
200g finely shredded savoy cabbage
1 small white onion (80g), chopped finely

Cook potato for cabbage mash.
Cook bacon and onion in medium frying pan, stirring until onion softens. Remove from heat.
Using hands, combine worcestershire sauce, breadcrumbs, egg, parsley, mince and half of the barbecue sauce with bacon mixture in large bowl; shape mixture into eight rissoles.
Cook rissoles in same pan, in batches, until browned both sides and cooked through. Cover to keep warm.
Place stock and remaining sauce in same pan; bring to a boil. Stir in blended cornflour and water; cook, stirring, until gravy boils and thickens slightly.
Finish cabbage mash. Serve rissoles and cabbage mash topped with gravy.

cabbage mash Boil, steam or microwave potato until tender; drain. Mash potato with milk and butter until smooth; stir in cabbage and onion.

serves 4
per serving 18.3g fat; 2282kJ (546 cal)

pumpkin and spinach frittata

900g pumpkin, sliced thinly
2 cloves garlic, crushed
1 tablespoon olive oil
6 eggs
½ cup (125ml) cream
40g baby spinach leaves
¼ cup (20g) coarsely grated parmesan

Preheat oven to moderately hot (200°C/180°C fan-forced).
Place pumpkin, in single layer, on baking trays; brush with combined garlic and oil. Roast, uncovered, until tender.
Meanwhile, oil deep 20cm-square cake pan; line base and sides with baking paper.
Whisk eggs with cream in medium jug. Layer half of the pumpkin in prepared pan; pour half of the egg mixture over pumpkin. Top with spinach and remaining pumpkin, then pour over remaining egg mixture; sprinkle with cheese.
Bake, uncovered, about 25 minutes or until firm. Stand 5 minutes before cutting into triangles.

serves 4
per serving 28.5g fat; 1555kJ (370 cal)

sweet soy chicken with noodles

Kecap manis is an Indonesian sweet soy sauce that is available at most supermarkets and Asian-food stores. We used hokkien noodles in this recipe, but any fresh wheat noodle, such as shanghai, can be substituted.

500g hokkien noodles
1 tablespoon peanut oil
750g chicken thigh fillets, sliced thickly
8 green onions, chopped coarsely
4 cloves garlic, crushed
2cm piece fresh ginger (10g), sliced thinly
230g can sliced water chestnuts, drained
300g choy sum, chopped coarsely
2 tablespoons coarsely chopped fresh coriander
2 tablespoons kecap manis
¼ cup (60ml) chicken stock

Place noodles in medium heatproof bowl, cover with boiling water, separate with fork; drain. Cover to keep warm.
Heat oil in wok; stir-fry chicken, in batches, until browned all over. Return chicken to wok with onion, garlic, ginger and water chestnuts; stir-fry until fragrant.
Add choy sum, coriander, kecap manis and stock; stir-fry until chicken is cooked through and choy sum just wilted.
Serve noodles topped with chicken mixture.

serves 4
per serving 20g fat; 2761kJ (659 cal)
tip Chilli lovers may like to serve this dish with sambal oelek.

sang choy bow

1 tablespoon sesame oil
1 medium brown onion (150g), chopped finely
2 cloves garlic, crushed
300g pork mince
300g veal mince
¼ cup (60ml) soy sauce
¼ cup (60ml) oyster sauce
1 medium red capsicum (150g), chopped finely
3 cups (240g) bean sprouts
3 green onions, chopped coarsely
1 tablespoon toasted sesame seeds
8 large iceberg lettuce leaves

Heat oil in wok; stir-fry brown onion and garlic until onion softens. Add both minces; stir-fry until cooked through.
Add sauces and capsicum, reduce heat; simmer, uncovered, stirring occasionally, 3 minutes.
Just before serving, stir in sprouts, green onion and seeds. Divide lettuce leaves among serving plates; spoon sang choy bow into leaves.

serves 4
per serving 17.2g fat; 1463kJ (350 cal)

salmon with grilled corn salsa

6 salmon fillets or cutlets (1.2kg)

corn salsa

2 trimmed corn cobs (500g)

2 medium red capsicums (400g)

1 small red onion (100g), chopped finely

1 fresh small red thai chilli, seeded, chopped finely

1 tablespoon olive oil

¼ cup chopped fresh coriander

Make corn salsa.

Cook salmon on heated oiled barbecue plate until browned both sides and cooked as desired.

Serve salmon with corn salsa and grilled bread, if desired.

corn salsa Cook corn on heated oiled barbecue plate, covered loosely with a piece of foil, about 20 minutes or until browned and tender. Using a sharp knife, cut kernels from cobs. Quarter capsicums; remove and discard seeds and membranes. Cook on heated oiled barbecue plate until skin blisters and blackens. Cover capsicum pieces with plastic or paper 5 minutes. Peel away and discard skin; chop capsicum flesh finely. Combine corn and capsicum with remaining ingredients.

serves 6

per serving 18.5g fat; 1766kJ (422 cal)

tips Corn salsa can be made 3 hours ahead. Salmon is best served a little rare in the centre, to keep texture moist.

lamb cutlets with roasted potatoes and tomatoes

500g new potatoes, quartered
2 tablespoons olive oil
250g grape tomatoes
12 lamb cutlets (900g)
½ cup loosely packed fresh basil leaves
½ cup loosely packed fresh flat-leaf parsley leaves
1 tablespoon balsamic vinegar

Preheat oven to hot (220°C/200°C fan-forced).
Toss potato and oil in large baking dish; roast, uncovered, 15 minutes. Add tomatoes; roast, uncovered, about 10 minutes or until potato is tender.
Meanwhile, cook lamb on heated oiled grill plate (or grill or barbecue) until browned both sides and cooked as desired.
Place potato mixture and remaining ingredients in medium bowl; toss gently to combine. Serve lamb on potato mixture.

serves 4
per serving 28.9g fat; 1818kJ (434 cal)

rice paper rolls

You will need twelve 17cm-square rice paper sheets for this recipe.

Thinly slice ½ lebanese cucumber and ½ medium carrot into ribbons. Combine with 2 tablespoons hoi sin sauce, 1¼ cups finely shredded barbecued chicken and 50g thinly sliced snow peas. Place a sheet of rice paper in bowl of warm water until just softened; lift from water, place on tea-towel-covered board with a corner point towards you. Place a tablespoon of chicken mixture horizontally in centre of rice paper. Roll sheet to enclose filling, folding in sides as you go.

makes 12
per roll 0.8g fat; 160kJ (38 cal)

hummus

Blend or process two 300g cans rinsed drained chickpeas with 2 tablespoons tahini, ⅓ cup (80ml) lemon juice, two quartered cloves garlic and ¼ cup (60ml) water until almost smooth. With motor operating, gradually add ½ cup (125ml) olive oil in a thin, steady stream until mixture forms a smooth paste.

makes 2¼ cups
per tablespoon 5.6g fat; 263kJ (63 cal)

guacamole

Mash three medium avocados in medium bowl; stir in half a finely chopped small red onion, one seeded finely chopped small egg tomato, 1 tablespoon lime juice and ¼ cup coarsely chopped fresh coriander.

makes **2½ cups**
per tablespoon 4g fat; 157kJ (38 cal)

tuna salad on focaccia melt

Combine half a drained 185g can tuna in brine, 2 tablespoons mayonnaise, half a finely chopped small red onion and 2 tablespoons finely chopped fresh flat-leaf parsley in small bowl. Cut a 300g garlic focaccia into quarters; spread tuna mixture over one quarter, top with one slice of tasty cheese. Place under preheated grill about 5 minutes or until cheese melts.

makes **1**
per melt 23.9g fat; 2160kJ (516 cal)

antipasto pizza melt

Spread 1 tablespoon sun-dried tomato pesto over small pizza base; top with 4 drained marinated artichoke quarters, 30g drained bottled char-grilled capsicum and ¼ cup (25g) coarsely grated mozzarella cheese. Place under preheated grill about 5 minutes or until cheese melts.

makes 1
per melt 26.4g fat; 4328kJ (1034 cal)

salmon and cucumber open bagel

Discard skin and bones from a quarter of a drained 210g can red salmon. Combine salmon in small bowl with a quarter of a seeded finely chopped lebanese cucumber, 1 teaspoon lemon juice and 1 tablespoon sour cream. Spread 1 tablespoon cream cheese over half of a bagel; top with salmon mixture.

makes 1
per bagel 18.5g fat; 1523kJ (364 cal)

mixed berry crumpet

Combine ½ cup (160g) raspberry jam with 1½ cups (225g) thawed mixed frozen berries. Spoon onto 8 crumpets; serve with 1 cup (280g) yogurt.

makes **8**
per crumpet 1.8g fat; 635kJ (152 cal)

beetroot dip

Blend or process 850g can drained beetroot slices, one quartered clove garlic, ¼ cup (60g) sour cream, 1 tablespoon tahini and 1 tablespoon lemon juice until smooth.

makes **2½ cups**
per tablespoon 1.3g fat; 86kJ (21 cal)

fruit scrolls

40g butter
¼ teaspoon ground nutmeg
1½ tablespoons brown sugar
2 teaspoons ground cinnamon
1 small apple (130g), peeled, cored, grated coarsely
⅓ cup (50g) finely chopped dried apricots
½ cup (125ml) orange juice
1 sheet ready-rolled puff pastry

Preheat oven to moderately hot (200°C/180°C fan-forced). Lightly grease oven tray.
Melt half of the butter in small saucepan; add nutmeg, sugar and cinnamon. Cook, stirring, over low heat, until sugar dissolves. Stir in apple, apricot and half of the juice; bring to a boil. Reduce heat; simmer, uncovered, 2 minutes. Remove from heat; stir in remaining juice.
Spread fruit mixture over pastry sheet; roll into log. Cut log into quarters; place on prepared tray, 5cm apart, brush with remaining melted butter.
Bake, uncovered, about 20 minutes or until scrolls are cooked through.
Serve hot scrolls with vanilla yogurt or low-fat custard and dusted with sifted icing sugar, if desired.

serves 4
per serving 19.2g fat; 1442kJ (344 cal)

fruit skewers with honey yogurt

½ medium pineapple (625g)
2 large oranges (600g)
250g strawberries
2 large bananas (460g)
30g butter
¼ cup (55g) brown sugar
1 tablespoon lemon juice
1 cup (280g) honey yogurt

Peel pineapple; cut away and discard core. Cut pineapple into 2.5cm lengths; cut lengths crossways into 3cm pieces.
Peel oranges thickly to remove bitter white pith; separate orange segments. Remove hulls from strawberries; cut in half lengthways. Peel bananas; cut into 3cm slices.
Thread fruit, alternating varieties, onto twelve 20cm wooden skewers; place on oven tray.
Combine butter, sugar and juice in small saucepan over low heat, stirring, until butter melts and sugar dissolves. Pour butter mixture over skewers, making sure all fruits are coated in mixture.
Cook skewers, in batches, on heated lightly greased grill plate (or grill or barbecue) about 5 minutes or until browned lightly.
Serve skewers with honey yogurt.

serves 4
per serving 8.5g fat; 1352kJ (323 cal)
tip Soak the skewers in cold water for at least an hour before using to prevent them splintering and scorching.

mango and raspberry jelly

425g can sliced mango
85g packet mango jelly crystals
2 cups (500ml) boiling water
150g raspberries
85g packet raspberry jelly crystals
1 cup (250ml) cold water
300ml thickened cream

Drain mango in sieve over small bowl; reserve 1 cup mango liquid. Measure ¼ cup mango slices and reserve. Divide remaining mango slices among eight ¾-cup (180ml) glasses.
Combine mango jelly crystals with 1 cup of the boiling water in small bowl, stirring until jelly dissolves; stir in reserved mango liquid. Divide evenly among glasses over mango, cover; refrigerate about 2 hours or until jelly sets.
Divide raspberries among glasses over jelly. Combine raspberry jelly crystals and remaining cup of the boiling water in small bowl, stirring until jelly dissolves; stir in the cold water. Divide evenly among glasses over raspberries, cover; refrigerate about 2 hours or until jelly sets.
Beat cream in small bowl with electric mixer until soft peaks form. Using rubber spatula, spread cream equally among glasses; top with reserved mango slices.

serves 8
per serving 13.9g fat; 1022kJ (244 cal)
tip If mangoes are in season, you can use one large fresh mango weighing about 600g for this recipe. Peel the mango over a small bowl to catch as much juice as possible; cut off mango cheeks, slice thinly. Squeeze as much juice as possible from around mango seed into bowl; add enough cold water to make 1 cup of liquid to be added to the mango jelly crystals (see step 2).

muesli slice

125g butter
⅓ cup (75g) firmly packed brown sugar
2 tablespoons honey
1 cup (90g) rolled oats
½ cup (45g) desiccated coconut
½ cup (80g) finely chopped dried apricots
½ cup (75g) finely chopped dried apples
½ cup (80g) sultanas
½ cup (75g) self-raising flour

Preheat oven to moderate (180°C/160°C fan-forced). Grease and line a 20cm x 30cm slice pan.
Combine butter, sugar and honey in large saucepan; stir over medium heat, without boiling, until sugar dissolves. Remove from heat; stir in remaining ingredients.
Press mixture into pan. Bake, uncovered, about 20 minutes or until golden brown. Cool in pan; cut into squares to serve.

makes **20**
per serve 7.1g fat; 589kJ (141 cal)

apple and berry crumble

800g can pie apple
2 cups (300g) frozen mixed berries
1 tablespoon white sugar
½ cup (125ml) water
1 cup (120g) toasted muesli
2 tablespoons plain flour
1 tablespoon brown sugar
50g butter
½ cup (20g) corn flakes

Preheat oven to moderate (180°C/160°C fan-forced).
Combine apple, berries, white sugar and the water in medium saucepan; bring to a boil. Reduce heat; simmer, stirring, until mixture is combined. Remove from heat.
Meanwhile, combine muesli, flour and brown sugar in medium bowl. Use fingertips to rub in butter; stir in corn flakes.
Place apple mixture in 2-litre (8-cup) ovenproof dish; sprinkle with muesli mixture. Bake, uncovered, about 20 minutes or until browned lightly. Serve with cream, if desired.

serves 6
per serve 9.1g fat; 1037kJ (248 cal)

apricot and coconut muffins

425g can apricot halves
2¼ cups (335g) self-raising flour
¾ cup (165g) firmly packed brown sugar
1 egg
⅔ cup (160ml) buttermilk
½ cup (125ml) vegetable oil
⅓ cup (110g) apricot jam

coconut topping

¼ cup (35g) plain flour
1 tablespoon caster sugar
⅓ cup (25g) shredded coconut
30g butter

Preheat oven to moderate (180°C/160°C fan-forced). Grease 12-hole (⅓-cup/80ml) muffin pan.
Drain apricots, discard syrup; chop apricots coarsely.
Make coconut topping.
Combine flour and sugar in large bowl; use a fork to stir in apricot, then combined egg, buttermilk, oil and jam. Mixture should look lumpy, do not over-mix.
Divide mixture among pan holes; sprinkle coconut topping over each muffin mixture. Bake, uncovered, about 25 minutes. Stand muffins in pan 5 minutes; turn, top-side up, onto wire rack to cool.
coconut topping Combine flour, sugar and coconut in small bowl; use fingers to rub butter into flour mixture.

makes 12
per muffin 14.1g fat; 1346kJ (322 cal)

mini carrot and pineapple cakes

⅓ cup (50g) plain flour
½ cup (75g) self-raising flour
½ teaspoon bicarbonate of soda
¼ cup (55g) caster sugar
½ teaspoon ground cinnamon
225g can crushed pineapple, drained
⅔ cup (160g) firmly packed finely grated carrot
⅓ cup (80ml) vegetable oil
1 egg, beaten lightly

cream cheese icing
125g cream cheese, softened
1 tablespoon icing sugar
1 teaspoon lemon juice
2 teaspoons milk

Preheat oven to moderate (180°C/160°C fan-forced). Grease two 12-hole (1 tablespoon/20ml) mini muffin pans.
Sift flours, soda, sugar and cinnamon into bowl. Add pineapple and carrot; stir in combined oil and egg (do not over-mix).
Divide mixture among pan holes. Bake about 15 minutes. Stand muffins in pans 5 minutes; turn onto wire rack to cool.
Meanwhile, make cream cheese icing.
Spread cooled muffins with icing.
cream cheese icing Combine ingredients in small bowl.

makes 24
per cake 5.1g fat; 343kJ (82 cal)

frozen yogurt and raspberry swirl

⅔ cup (150g) caster sugar
⅓ cup (80ml) water
1 teaspoon gelatine
120g frozen raspberries, thawed
500g thick Greek-style yogurt

Combine sugar and the water in small saucepan, stir over low heat until sugar dissolves; cool 5 minutes. Sprinkle gelatine over syrup; stir until gelatine dissolves.
Push raspberries through fine sieve over bowl; discard seeds.
Combine gelatine mixture and yogurt in medium bowl; pour into 14cm x 21cm loaf pan. Cover; freeze about 4 hours or until almost firm.
Uncover, scrape yogurt from bottom and sides of pan with fork; swirl raspberry through yogurt. Cover; freeze until ready to serve. Serve with fresh raspberries, if desired.

serves 6
per serve 5.9g fat; 865kJ (207 cal)

glossary

baby corn small corn cobs canned in brine, available from most Asian food stores.

bacon rashers also known as bacon slices; made from cured and smoked pork side.

bagel small ring-shaped bread roll with a dense, chewy texture and shiny crust. Bagels are boiled in water before they're 'baked'.

bean sprouts also known as bean shoots; tender new growths of assorted beans and seeds germinated for consumption as sprouts. The most readily available are mung bean, soy bean, alfalfa and snow pea sprouts.

butter use salted or unsalted (sweet) butter; 125g is equal to 1 stick butter.

capsicum also known as bell pepper or, simply, pepper. Native to Central and South America, they can be red, green, yellow, orange or purplish black. Seeds and membranes should be discarded before use.

cheese

cheddar the most common cow milk 'tasty' cheese; should be aged, hard and have a pronounced bite.

cream commonly known as Philadelphia or Philly, a soft cow milk cheese with a fat content of at least 33%. Sold at supermarkets.

fetta Greek in origin; a crumbly textured goat or sheep milk cheese with a sharp, salty taste.

parmesan also known as parmigiano, parmesan is a hard, grainy cow milk cheese that originated in the Parma region of Italy. The curd is salted in brine for a month before being aged for up to two years in humid conditions. Parmesan is mainly grated as a topping for pasta, soups and other savoury dishes, but is also delicious eaten with fruit.

chilli, thai small, medium hot, and bright red in colour.

choy sum also known as pakaukeo or flowering cabbage, a member of the bok choy family; easy to identify with its long stems, light green leaves and yellow flowers. Is eaten, stems and all, steamed or stir-fried.

coconut

desiccated unsweetened, concentrated, finely dried coconut.

shredded dried thin strips.

corn flakes crisp flakes of corn.

cornflour also known as cornstarch; used as a thickening agent in cooking.

eggplant also known as aubergine; belongs to the same family as tomatoes, chillies and potatoes. Ranging in size from tiny to very large and in colour from pale green to deep purple, eggplant has an equally wide variety of flavours.

flour, plain an all-purpose flour, made from wheat.

garlic salt mixture of fine garlic powder and free-running table salt.

gelatine we used powdered gelatine; also available in sheet form known as leaf gelatine.

green onions also known as scallions or (incorrectly) shallots; immature onions picked before the bulbs have formed, having long, edible, bright-green stalks.

grill, griller broil, broiler.

herbs when specified, we used dried (not ground) herbs in the proportion of one to four for fresh herbs; eg, 1 teaspoon dried herbs equals 4 teaspoons (1 tablespoon) chopped fresh herbs.

coriander also known as pak chee, cilantro or chinese parsley; bright-green-leafed herb with a pungent flavour. Often stirred into or sprinkled over a dish just before serving for maximum impact. Both the stems and roots of coriander are also used in Thai cooking; wash well before chopping.

flat-leaf parsley also known as continental parsley or Italian parsley.

hummus a Middle-Eastern salad or dip made from softened dried chickpeas, garlic, lemon juice and tahini (sesame seed paste); can be purchased, ready-made, from most delicatessens and supermarkets.

iceberg lettuce a heavy, firm round crisp lettuce with tightly packed leaves.

jam also known as preserve or conserve; most often made from fruit.

lebanese cucumber short, slender and thin-skinned; this variety is also known as the european or burpless cucumber.

maple syrup a thin syrup distilled from the sap of the maple tree. Maple-flavoured syrup or pancake syrup is not an adequate substitute for the real thing.

milk we used full-cream homogenised milk unless otherwise specified.

buttermilk sold alongside fresh milk products in supermarkets and is commercially made, by a method similar to yogurt. Despite the implication of its name, it is low in fat and is a good substitute for dairy products such as cream or sour cream, good in baking and in salad dressings.

mince also known as ground meat.

mustard, dijon a pale brown, distinctively flavoured fairly mild French mustard.

noodles, bean thread also known as wun sen, made from extruded mung bean paste; also known as cellophane or glass noodles because they are transparent when cooked. White in colour (not off-white like rice vermicelli), very delicate and fine; available dried in various size bundles. Must be soaked to soften before use; using them deep-fried requires no pre-soaking.

paprika ground dried red capsicum (bell pepper), available sweet or hot.

pepitas dried pumpkin seeds.

pumpkin sometimes used interchangeably with the word squash, the pumpkin is a member of the gourd family and is used in cooking both as one of many ingredients in a dish or eaten on its own. Various types can be substituted for one another.

raisins dried sweet grapes.

ready-rolled puff pastry packaged sheets of frozen puff pastry, available from supermarkets.

rice paper sheets made from rice paste and stamped into brittle rounds. Dipped in water they become pliable wrappers.

rocket also known as arugula, rugula and rucola; a peppery-tasting green leaf which can be used similarly to baby spinach leaves, eaten raw in salads or used in cooking. Baby rocket leaves are both smaller and less peppery.

sauces

barbecue a spicy, tomato-based sauce used to marinate, baste or as an accompaniment.

fish called naam pla if it is Thai made; the Vietnamese version, nuoc naam, is almost identical. Made from pulverised salted fermented fish (most often anchovies); has a pungent smell and strong taste. There are many versions of varying intensity, so use according to taste.

hoisin a thick, sweet and spicy chinese paste made from salted fermented soy beans, onions and garlic; used as a marinade or baste, or to accent stir-fries and barbecued or roasted foods.

kecap manis dark, thick sweet soy sauce used in most South-East Asian cuisines. Depending on the brand, the soy's sweetness is derived from the addition of either molasses or palm sugar when brewed.

oyster Asian in origin, this rich, brown sauce is made from oysters and their brine, cooked with salt and soy sauce, and thickened with starches.

snow peas also called mange tout ('eat all'). Snow pea tendrils, the growing shoots of the plant, are sold by green grocers.

sugar we used coarse, granulated table sugar, also known as crystal sugar, unless otherwise specified.

brown an extremely soft, fine granulated sugar retaining molasses for its characteristic colour and flavour.

caster also known as finely granulated or superfine sugar.

icing sugar also known as confectioners' sugar or powdered sugar.

sultanas also known as golden raisins; dried, seedless white grapes.

tahini sesame seed paste available from Middle-Eastern food stores; most often used in hummus, baba ghanoush and other Lebanese recipes.

tomatoes

canned whole peeled tomatoes in natural juices.

egg also called plum or Roma, these are smallish, oval-shaped tomatoes much used in Italian cooking or salads.

zucchini also known as courgette.

index

facts & figures

These conversions are approximate only, but the difference between an exact and the approximate conversion of various liquid and dry measures is minimal and will not affect your cooking results.

Note: NZ, Canada, US and UK all use 15ml tablespoons. Australian tablespoons measure 20ml. All cup and spoon measurements are level.

Measuring equipment

The difference between one country's measuring cups and another's is, at most, within a 2 or 3 teaspoon variance. (For the record, 1 Australian metric measuring cup holds approximately 250ml.) The most accurate way of measuring dry ingredients is to weigh them. For liquids, use a clear glass or plastic jug having metric markings.

How to measure

When using graduated measuring cups, shake dry ingredients loosely into the appropriate cup. Do not tap the cup on a bench or tightly pack the ingredients unless directed to do so. Level the top of measuring cups and measuring spoons with a knife. When measuring liquids, place a clear glass or plastic jug having metric markings on a flat surface to check accuracy at eye level.

Dry measures

metric	imperial
15g	½oz
30g	1oz
60g	2oz
90g	3oz
125g	4oz (¼lb)
155g	5oz
185g	6oz
220g	7oz
250g	8oz (½lb)
280g	9oz
315g	10oz
345g	11oz
375g	12oz (¾lb)
410g	13oz
440g	14oz
470g	15oz
500g	16oz (1lb)
750g	24oz (1½lb)
1kg	32oz (2lb)

We use large eggs with an average weight of 60g.

Liquid measures

metric	imperial
30 ml	1 fluid oz
60 ml	2 fluid oz
100 ml	3 fluid oz
125 ml	4 fluid oz
150 ml	5 fluid oz (¼ pint/1 gill)
190 ml	6 fluid oz
250 ml (1cup)	8 fluid oz
300 ml	10 fluid oz (½ pint)
500 ml	16 fluid oz
600 ml	20 fluid oz (1 pint)
1000 ml (1litre)	1¾ pints

Helpful measures

metric	imperial
3mm	⅛in
6mm	¼in
1cm	½in
2cm	¾in
2.5cm	1in
6cm	2½in
8cm	3in
20cm	8in
23cm	9in
25cm	10in
30cm	12in (1ft)

Oven temperatures

These oven temperatures are only a guide for conventional ovens. For fan-forced ovens, check the manufacturer's manual.

	°C (Celsius)	°F (Fahrenheit)	Gas Mark
Very slow	120	250	½
Slow	150	275-300	1-2
Moderately slow	170	325	3
Moderate	180	350-375	4-5
Moderately hot	200	400	6
Hot	220	425-450	7-8
Very hot	240	475	9